The Unflattering Sweater

Overcoming Strongholds to Find Truth

Lisa R. Davis-Wall

TTL PUBLISHING

WAKE FOREST, NORTH CAROLINA

The Unflattering Sweater by Lisa R. Davis-Wall
TTL Publishing
P.O. Box 1744
Wake Forest, North Carolina 27588
info@tokunbotheleader.com
Visit the publisher's website at tokunbotheleader.com.

Visit the author's website at mustardseedworks.com.
Cover Design by Darius Carr.

Unless otherwise noted, all scriptures are taken from the New International Version Bible, New King James Version Bible, and New Living Translation Bible.

The Unflattering Sweater/Lisa R. Davis-Wall
ISBN: 978-1-7378576-3-1

My very first book is dedicated to my mommy, Gloria C. Davis, who was a living example of the value of repurposing. She was one of the most creative people I knew. She definitely had the knack of turning what others considered to be trash into beautiful treasures. I learned very early in life that people, like things, can also be utilized in more than one way throughout their lives. In our lifetime together, I watched her reinvent herself to become a better version of herself over and over again. I also heard her speak life into people. She had the ability to cast a new vision for the future into people that others had given up on, including me.

Thank you, Mommy, for never being in a hurry to throw something or people away simply because it or they no longer fit the original purpose in your life. My only regret is that you are not here to read this! I know you would have been so proud. I love you, Mommy. Rest in His arms.

Love always,

Your Chalupa

CONTENTS

Foreword by Pastors Bernard and Tina McNeill from New Life Fellowship in Rochester, New York

Pastor Bernard's Thoughts

I have had the privilege to serve as Lisa's senior pastor for the past four years. It has been a great joy to witness how God has continued to allow us all to experience true and tangible blessings as a result of this connection. Lisa serves as an elder where she oversees the ministry of prayer and intercession. Although she leads within a specific area of ministry, her many gifts have blessed the lives of New Life Fellowship far beyond the ordained assignment. Her willingness to step "in-between" for the benefit of others is a genuine gift. She can miraculously relate, connect, and empathize with those who are seeking help. This gift allows her to minister from a very personal and authentic place. Lisa is considered to be the one who is steady and unwavering. Her tone is calm and her words are reliable. She is a relentless and skilled kingdom warrior and highly esteemed by her leadership, peers, family, and community.

In The Unflattering Sweater, Lisa's compelling insight (rich in wisdom and experience) inspires one's faith to increase. Her story causes people to be open and willing to trust God in their transformation process. Lisa's story, which is shared so freely, will remind you of the plan and life blueprint God has for all of us. The story she tells highlights God's plan to prosper us, and not to harm us, to give us hope and a future. She shares a very powerful and yet practical approach to assist in the discovery of "life layers." With the knitting of the sweater comes a story of how life is full of God-given purpose, just waiting to be discovered.

Pastor Tina's Thoughts

As you journey through The Unflattering Sweater, I can assure you that you will immediately fall in love with the honesty and authenticity of the author. In addition, there will be a reckoning within you identifying with the realities of pain, suffering, courage, wellness, and redemption.

Similar to experiencing the wonder of a five-course meal allowing for seconds, the reader is presented with elements of surprise throughout each course utilizing the developed (or under-developed) palette to distinguish which flavors are worth incorporating into a personalized list of must-have (or, no thanks) menu items.

The author undoubtedly provides us with a navigation tool to help us receive victory over circumstances that were meant to destroy our lives. Through the use of scriptural truths, substantive analogies, and applicable prayer guides, The Unflattering Sweater gives people an understanding that we can triumph through painful moments. Regardless of age, gender, socio-economic status, or religious belief, The Unflattering Sweater will impact your heart and prayerfully, bless your life as never before.

Introduction

The Call of God

God gave me the idea to write this book about ten years ago. It has taken me a while to finally complete this book for many reasons. At first, I was hesitant to share a story about my authentic journey of healing after my divorce. I also wanted to incorporate how knitting a sweater was a concept that God used to bring me into a place of redemption. The concept was kind of quirky, it didn't sound overly deep or mystical, and I thought it would be easy. Unfortunately, I waited to finish this book because of procrastination, fear, hesitation, and other destiny thieves that came along and pushed away my obedience to finish this book. Eventually, the Holy Spirit pushed through my fears and sort of gave me an ultimatum to complete this book.

The call of God to act on His behalf can come at odd times. We never really know when we may hear the voice of the Lord, or under what circumstances. For many of us, there is a crystalline moment, a moment when His call meets our circumstances, and our assignment and mandate are given. I remember when God confirmed the necessity and the urgency of having to share this particular story. It was during a time when I was preparing to speak during a "Women's Refresher" at our church. My topic was, God Hears. I decided to speak about the biblical character, Hagar, and how she came to know the God that hears. It would be my first time speaking on a platform of that magnitude. It was also the first time that I publicly shared with others about my divorce. I was nervous and struggled with the idea of sharing such a private story, but I felt the guidance of the Holy Spirit to do so.

Before this event, God sent me the confirmation that it was time to share my testimony of healing after a divorce through my interaction with a man that I was working with that I will call Bob. He was a 30-something, white man. To me, he seemed to be very emotionally detached. He was a great clinician and was all about business. We were friendly, but not friends, as was the case with most of the Caucasian men that I worked with.

One day, Bob asked me if I had a few minutes to talk. I was in the middle of something but said I would be available in a bit. We went to a vacant office, and he asked me to shut the door. He then began to tell me the story of how he found out that his wife was having an affair. My heart sank, and I began to weep internally for him. Then he said this: "I don't know anything about divorce. I don't know anyone personally that has been divorced. I do not know what to do, but I understand that you do. Will you help me?"

God brought this interaction back to my memory to highlight to me that it was time to write this book. I heard the call, but I didn't fully grasp the "why" behind it until this moment with Bob. Through this conversation with Bob, God changed everything that I thought I knew about this assignment. I had in mind that my audience would be mostly Christian women of color, of a certain age range, but there was this white, young, non-religious, man coming to me for assistance. He needed to hear my testimony. He needed me to be a guide. He needed to tap into my personal experience, and it was imperative for me to help him.

Getting Over Myself

For me to be used by God, I had to get over my embarrassment and questions about who was discussing my personal life. Sharing my story meant that I had to unlearn the wrong teaching that made me feel inadequate and ill-prepared to speak into a male's life. Pain and shared experience transcend race and gender. Most importantly, I needed to silence the voice of the enemy in my mind telling me I was inadequately prepared to offer any insight into this or any other situation. God was stretching my understanding of the call on my life and leading me into His Kingdom work.

Bob and I had the first of what would be many candid conversations as he walked through the dissolution of his marriage. After that brief period, we never spoke of it again. At that time, I was planted near Bob to speak life to him during a specific season in his life. I fulfilled the assignment that God ordained for me at that time. When I see Bob today, he appears to be thriving, and that is all that matters. My experience with Bob has given me the courage to help others work towards receiving the same type of victory. I want people to have the hope that there is life after great disappointment.

We Can Experience Victory

This book is for people who have come to difficult crossroads in their life. A difficult crossroad is a place where they have discovered that the best-laid plans do often go awry. This work is for those who have crafted their identity around someone or something and have discovered a shift in their foundation. This shift in their foundation now has them scrambling because the earth has moved under their feet. Who they thought they knew or trusted no longer is there to shape their identity.

This book is here to remind us that loss, even great loss, does not have to be the end of our story. In fact, it can be the beginning of more than we ever imagined or thought for our life. What would our life be like if we could start again? What could our life be like if we sought the original intent that the Creator God had for our lives and began to run after it? Starting again is a process of making one positive decision after another until we reach our goals. This process of discovering our authentic identity requires that we commit to doing something different and submit ourselves to God's processing. We cannot move on until we process what has happened in pain, and begin to see it in its correct perspective. It is only at that point that we can become something new.

I pray that this book blesses you. I pray that it ministers deliverance or freedom to you no matter what season of life you are in. I hope that this story will leave you refreshed, restored, and reassured that He who has begun a good work in you is faithful and can be trusted to complete it.

Now, grab a cup of tea, a slice of pound cake, and a comfortable seat. I want to share a cautionary tale about a sweater that I knit while I was recovering from divorce and the opportunity for self-discovery and life lessons that the Holy Spirit provided along the way. Many obstacles and strongholds were standing between me and the life that God intended. The instruction I received while knitting this sweater helped to propel me to the place of wholeness I stand in today. I want to share the saga of this ill-fitting garment, and how the Holy Spirit used it to bring healing to not only my broken heart but also to my past and ultimately my future. Understanding what God was trying to show me through the process of knitting an unflattering sweater is what prepared me to be able to speak life and not bitterness into Bob's life when he came to seek my help on that day.

ONE

STRONGHOLDS KEEP US IN PAIN

"For us to heal from pain, we must know the strongholds or negative thinking patterns that continue to keep us from becoming the authentic versions of ourselves."

I have been a member of a Pentecostal church for more than 20 years. During this time, I completed significant training in prayer and deliverance ministry. One of the areas that we focus on in our training is the concept of strongholds. One of my anchor scriptures as an intercessor is 2 Corinthians 10:4, "For the weapons of our warfare are not carnal but mighty in God for pulling down strongholds" (The New King James Version Bible, 2020). At first, I believed that I had a thorough understanding of what strongholds meant, how they operated, and how to combat them. However, a very painful life experience served as an instrument to help me to truly understand the impact that unaddressed strongholds had on my life.

Throughout this story, I want to address how strongholds continued to keep me bound to pain. For us to heal from pain, we must know the strongholds or negative thinking patterns that continue to keep us from becoming the authentic versions of ourselves. A stronghold in the natural sense is defined as, a place that has been fortified to protect it against attack. In addition, strongholds are a place where a particular cause or belief is strongly defended or upheld. Strongholds are deeply entrenched beliefs in our thinking system that hinder us from having a quality relationship with God, people, and ourselves. Undealt with strongholds usually leads us into living a life of deception.

People living in biblical times understood the significance of the word, stronghold. During biblical times, fortified cities were generally built on high ground, and encircled by a strong outer wall. These strongholds had only one opening, the city gate. Furthermore, this definition brings to mind the city of Jericho, and how it was surrounded by the fortified stone wall. The inhabitants of the city found comfort in knowing that the protective wall, and the stronghold that it created, would keep out enemy combatants, the diseased, or anything else that the community had decided would disrupt the established order in the city. On the other hand, if you were a captive or a prisoner of war, being in a stronghold represented a loss of freedom and control over your life.

Apostle Paul explicates in 2 Corinthians 10:3-6 (NKJV):

> *"3 For though we walk in the flesh, we do not war according to the flesh. 4 For the weapons of our warfare are not carnal but mighty in God for pulling down strongholds, 5 casting down arguments and every high thing that exalts itself against the knowledge of God, bringing every thought into captivity to the obedience of Christ, 6 and being ready to punish all disobedience when your obedience is fulfilled."*

I have structured this book as a kind of devotional/novel hybrid, in that I will use my lived experience as an object lesson of sorts. I have a story to tell, but I also have a mission to accomplish—and that is to help readers, to have applicable examples of how strongholds manifest in life events. Each portion of the story will be followed by a section highlighting the wisdom and insight I gained about the strongholds that were in operation at that time. The goal is to move the concept of strongholds out of the "spiritual clouds" and place understanding of them firmly within our reach. We can begin to conquer these strongholds or negative thinking patterns when we can see, articulate, and understand them.

After the wisdom gained, I share a prayer that I would like you to repeat. It's not enough to identify the stronghold; we also have to come out of agreement with it. When we fall out of agreement with them, this means that we

TWO

THE STRONGHOLD OF MISPLACED IDENTITY

"It is when we turn inspection of our hearts over to Holy Spirit, that He can uncover the areas of our being that have been tainted by anxiety, doubt, and sin."

I come from a family that has had seasons of what I like to call, "messiness." These seasons include times where there was violence, pain, rage, and disaster. Unfortunately, messiness was common in the time and place that I grew up. It seemed like domestic violence was the norm, infidelity in marriage was accepted, and children growing up trying to manage emotions and situations far above their cognitive capability were to be expected. It was a strange time, and we learned some strange and toxic lessons.

When I was in 8th grade, my mother left my dad and moved my sisters and me into a house in another part of town. We had lived in a cold-water walk-up all of our lives, so to be in a house, with my own room was a George and Louise Jefferson type of come-up for me. After our move, life got better, and things normalized a bit. I started to feel like my life was being released from the messiness that had doggedly followed me up until that point.

Reflecting on the challenging conditions that I endured in my childhood has enabled me to identify the genesis of the many strongholds that plagued me into my adult years. Those old, difficult, and discouraging challenges formed my thought patterns, my belief system, and affected my actions for decades. I think back to how solitary my life was. It wasn't that I was devoid of companions; I grew up with two younger sisters and a large extended family. Even with plenty of people being around me, I still was solitary. Loneliness built a fortress around my heart and my mind. I wasn't allowed to invite school friends over to play, but to be honest I didn't want to. One of the reasons I did not care to have company is because of the setup of our apartment. Our apartment consisted of two large rooms. We had a kitchen and a long hallway that led to the bathroom. The first room served as a bedroom and the living room; therefore, when we first walked in the door, we saw a big double bed. It embarrassed me because it wasn't like other kids' homes, so I didn't push the issue of having friends over. As an adult, that pattern of embarrassment for people to come to my home continued. It was difficult for me to invite other people outside of my immediate family into my home. The anxiety of being judged for my housekeeping, my decorator skills (or lack thereof), or the quality of my home was paralyzing. I did not experience a breakthrough in that area until I was in my 40's and started hosting a women's life group for my church.

Furthermore, strongholds can be developed based on the environment and conditions we live in. My proclivity to always want to be alone was also based on how I grew up. Because the tenement was positioned in the center of downtown, we weren't allowed to go outside until the storefronts closed, and then we sat on the stoop. There was a community of people of color in another part of town, but we didn't live there. Those children played together and grew together, and although I was with them in school, I didn't develop the same quality of relationship. There is something about children growing together in neighborhoods. It helps to develop a "village within the village" that births relational cohesiveness. I didn't have the gift of that in my life. I was well-liked by schoolmates and had many "friends," but I wasn't able to develop the lifelong friendships that other adults enjoy. I had solitary hobbies, (reading and crafting). In addition, I was asthmatic, so I couldn't participate in group sports. We did not live in a neighborhood with other children; consequently, I couldn't develop those relationships. We spent our summers with my grandmother, so there were no summertime games and adventures with schoolmates for me. I have always thought that I was an introvert, but as I think about it, I can't help but wonder if that is my natural bent, or if I developed introversion due to my environment. When we are teenagers, that kind of self-discovery is neither taught nor expected. I didn't learn about the concept of spiritual strongholds until I was an adult. I had no concept of a spiritual enemy, or any understanding of how growing up in the way that I had would form the way that I viewed life or mold my sense of self.

Because I lacked a sense of true identity, when the boy next door expressed interest in me, I gladly responded to his advances. My ex-husband became my boyfriend at an early age, and he was my friend. We were inseparable. He became my hiding place and my strong tower. I found my identity in our relationship and was unable to see myself living a life separate from him. As an adult, I see how I made an idol of our relationship. The enemy capitalized on my area of vulnerability, my loneliness, and my need for companionship. He caused me to exalt my relationship above the knowledge of God. I was very involved in the church we attended up until I graduated from high school. I served as a member of the choir, usher, and Sunday school teacher. I learned a lot about the Word, but I didn't learn how to filter my life through the lens of the Word. I learned about serving and works, but I didn't learn about developing a relationship with God, or what it truly meant to accept Him as Lord over my life. That void of revelation left me open for error to come in and have its way. It was a recipe for failure, and it played itself out not too many years after that.

After my boyfriend and I finished high school, I went to college while he enlisted in the military. We separated for a while, and life went on, with its missteps and its mistakes. Later on, we found each other again. Before I knew it, I had a daughter and a husband. Then, another daughter, and finally a son. My life felt legitimate, justified, and whole. I felt like I was finally going to be fine and that I had escaped the messiness. I was in love with my husband; I had my children, and I thought I was okay. I found out soon that deception gave me this belief.

Unfortunately, before I could understand what was happening, it all went away, and I was divorced. I probably should have seen it coming from the beginning. What would one expect from two kids that were trying to be adults that had tons of unpacked familial baggage and no role models of what a marriage should be? We married too young, had children too soon, and tried to make a life with too few resources. It's a wonder we stayed together for as long as we did. I remember the day I signed the final divorce papers like it was yesterday. My children and I had been suffering from a stomach bug for a week. It was horrible, we just couldn't shake it. If one of us started feeling better, then another of us would get sick. My youngest daughter was the sickest of all, and I was exhausted from trying to care for her. I think I lost at least 10 pounds over that week. I was weak and drained; I remember that I needed to go downtown to pick up the packet of papers. I was wearing sweatpants and a leather jacket. On that day, I remember being so cold. I was swimming in my clothes from the weight loss and the wind was whipping. I walked out of the County Clerk's Office onto Main Street with the packet in hand and just started to weep. The weight of failure washed over me like a tsunami. I was so ashamed and embarrassed. I felt like I had disappointed God and broken my covenant with Him. Loneliness and fear of how I was going to manage my life and that of my children left me breathless on that street corner. I'm not even sure how I made it back to my car. I went home, and life continued.

I spent the next few years in a crazy type of limbo. The dysfunction and poor examples from my childhood came back to haunt me. I was divorced from this man, and he was living his own life, but I still was allowing him to be entangled in mine. I could not disconnect from him. As I look back on that portion of my life, I fully understand what is meant by a "soul tie." My soul (mind, will, and emotions) was tied to that man. It was difficult to let Him go. I couldn't let go of the possibility that he would change his mind and want me back. After all, we were high school sweethearts! Everybody in town knew that we were together and that one day we would be married! I tried to position myself favorably before him. I accepted whatever crumbs of kindness and affection he would give me. Any little hint of favor in his eyes was like a gentle breath blowing over the embers of my heart, and that little flame that I protected so ferociously would rise and glow once again. It was pitiful and sad. I was pitiful and sad.

My ex-husband and I continued in this perverted dance for a few years. It seemed normal and acceptable to me because I had seen that same scenario played out in other relationships I observed growing up. It was normalized dysfunction. He had a few different relationships, and I kept holding on, thinking one of these days he's going to see me in a different light. With this unhealthy connection, something internally happened to me. We all know the saying, "there's a thin line between love and hate." Well, I'm here to testify that is the whole truth. I soon found myself crossing that line. I have no insight into psychology; therefore, I can't begin to diagnose the phenomenon I was exhibiting. I thought I loved him, and I thought I wanted to be with him, but I no longer was willing to change anything about myself to try to get him to love me back. It's like I was fully determined that he was going to take me back just the way I was. I felt like I had paid all of the penalties and gotten none of the prizes. This left me infuriated. The rage that I saw my father use against my mother rose in me. If I am to be honest, I think there were moments when I could have murdered him. I at least would have hit him with my car! I was sick of him, sick of his girlfriends, and sick of his inconsistency with our children, or at least I was on that day. If you asked me the next day, I would have told you that I wanted him back, and the cold, dead embers would flare up again. Even though he was painfully honest with me, and told me not to get my hopes up, I would get my hopes up again.

Imagine my reaction when he told me that he was remarrying! Before I could wrap my mind around that, I found out that he was married. Not that he was getting married - that he was married. To top it off, he had married a woman in our church! The pain of loss gripped my heart like a vice. I felt like the air was burning in my chest, and each breath felt short and ragged. I looked around me and saw the pain in the eyes of my children and something vital in me broke. The earth had shifted under my feet.

WISDOM GAINED

All of us are a composite of our life experiences, our struggles, and our triumphs. The conglomeration of all of those elements creates our perspectives. It dictates how we both define and feel about our individual lives and how we express our identity. We can be deceived by our feelings. The enemy of our soul studies our lives to know our vulnerabilities and take advantage of them. He is indeed like that lion, prowling about to see whom he can devour. If we live a life led by our emotions and not by the Spirit of God, we can easily fall prey to his devices.

Psalm 139:23-24 (NKJV) says, "Search me O God, and know my heart; test me and know my anxious thoughts. See if there is any offensive way in me and lead me in the way everlasting."

Self-examination is something that we should do regularly, but it usually doesn't happen until we are forced to by unexpected life events. Living an unexamined life is reckless and unwise. My childhood was a setup for the missteps that I would take later in life. Because I had not been taught who I was in Christ, and to apprehend the plan and the purpose that He has for me, I was ill-equipped to combat the lies of the enemy. We think we know ourselves and understand our motives, but even the scriptures attest to the untruth of that belief. Jeremiah 17:9 states, The heart is deceitful above all things and beyond cure. Who can understand it? (New International Version of the Bible, 2011)

Often, the enemy uses pride to distort our vision of ourselves. Pride causes us to be puffed up; it hides our offenses and inhibits our ability to see the true condition of our hearts.

None of us want to see ourselves as the villain in our own story. It is so much easier to blame someone else for our hurt and our disappointments. The concept that we sometimes partner with the architect of our missteps can be a difficult pill to swallow, but it is necessary if we are to see ourselves in a true light.

It is when we turn inspection of our hearts over to Holy Spirit, that He can uncover the areas of our being that have been tainted by anxiety, doubt, and sin. It is then that He can order our steps and lead us into the way everlasting.

PRAYER

Father God, thank you for searching my heart and knowing me. You stand outside of time and can see all of my days. You know my heart, my motives, my struggles. and all of my joys. Help me to guard my heart, as all that I do springs from it. Give me a heart posture that glorifies you and reflects your love and your mercy. In the places where I fail, I ask that you create in me a clean heart and a contrite spirit. I choose to make your Word the plumbline against which I measure my thoughts, my emotions, and my motives. I submit myself to the leading of the Holy Spirit and commit to walking circumspectly before You. Help me to get to know you better, and as I learn more of You, enable me to discover more about myself. You created and formed me for a reason. Your Word declares that I am made in Your image, I'm a little lower than the angels, and that You crowned me with glory and honor. Guide me by Your Spirit in my journey to understanding my Kingdom identity and purpose in the earth. As I seek after you, may Your peace, which transcends all understanding, guard my heart and mind in Christ Jesus. This is my earnest desire. In Jesus' name. Amen.

SCRIPTURE FOR MEDITATION

1 John 3:1 (NIV)

See what great love the Father has lavished on us, that we should be called children of God! And that is what we are! The reason the world does not know us is that it did not know him.

THREE

THE STRONGHOLDS OF REJECTION AND DOUBT

"Our trust in God and the faith that it builds is what extinguishes the fiery dart of doubt and renders it powerless."

When I was a child, I suffered from exercise-induced asthma. It's part of the reason that I trained as a Respiratory Therapist. I have practiced for over 30 years. In the '70s, children with asthma were not allowed to run and play because it would bring on "asthma attacks" - exacerbations of wheezing and coughing. Hand-held inhalers were not yet common, so exacerbations away from medical assistance could be deadly. This affected what I could and could not do as a child. My family and I spent several summers with our grandmother in Monticello, Georgia. I was allowed to play in the yard with the other children for a while each day. If my wheezing flared up, I would be relegated back to the porch to sit and catch my breath.

Those times of sitting on the porch with my mom and other ladies were the genesis of my love of handcrafting. The first skill I acquired was embroidery. I spent many hot and humid days on my grandmother's porch embroidering flowers, birds, ducklings, and swirls on pillowcases and the edges of bed sheets.

My mom primarily worked as a domestic for most of my childhood. One of the women that she worked for taught her to crochet. I became drawn to the possibility of creating something new, so my mom taught me to crochet. She taught me how to crochet everything from frilly doilies, sofa pillows, and afghans. I had an innate gift for deciphering and mastering complicated patterns. Soon I was teaching my mother and Aunt Lizz how to create some of the more intricate designs. I also was an avid reader, devouring books far above my grade level in record time. Reading and handcrafting became my place of solace. I could lose myself in a good book, or an intricate pattern, and the stress of living in a house where fists and angry words could spring up unexpectedly and disrupt the peace would ease. A book or a needle in my hand were my weapons of warfare against fear, anger, disappointment, and pain.

In my second year of college, I was hired as a resident advisor in my dormitory. We were tasked with welcoming our new residents with name tags on their doors, so I spent the summer break cross-stitching their names onto a fabric that I crafted into personalized door markers. One of my classmates, Fung Ying Kwong, taught me the basic knitting stitches, knit and purl. She was always knitting herself a new scarf, (which we desperately needed for those Syracuse winters) and I wanted to make a few for myself. I didn't move past the basics of scarf knitting at the time. I guess I was too busy with my studies and my social agenda. So, with that as my backdrop, it is understandable that handcrafting would come to my rescue during one of the most painful times of my life.

Finding out that my ex-husband had remarried devastated me and sent my life into a tailspin. I was all over the place. It was during this time that I needed to visit with Mrs. Boyd, my friend Leslie's mom, who lives in NYC. I was there for a conference and spent the night with her in Harlem. When I got there, I was a restless soul, and I couldn't get myself settled. After dinner, Mrs. Boyd sat down on the sofa and picked up the yarn and crochet needle that she had sitting in a bag by her seat. She was working on an afghan. "It helps me to relax," she said quietly. As I looked at her working away, she looked so peaceful, and at that moment I knew that I wanted that type of peace in my life again. When I returned home, I went to the local yarn shop in my neighborhood and picked up some yarn. I went to the Lion Brand yarn website, and downloaded the How to Knit eBook, and began to re-teach myself the basic stitches. My adventure of finding peace had begun.

I have never been one to just dip my toes in the water. Once I decide I'm doing something, I'm all in. Once I started relearning how to knit, it became all-encompassing. It was the distraction that I needed, and it started to take over all of my free time. I spent money that I didn't have on expensive yarns and specialty needles. I bought pattern leaflets and spent work time looking up and downloading patterns from the internet. It became my obsession. I started out making hats with double-pointed needles. I had never made anything in the round, and I was fascinated. I made all kinds of hats, with matching scarves and mittens. Everybody around me got a hat! I was working at a hospital, and I started teaching the ladies I was working with how to knit, and they started making hats! My obsession was so bad that some of our male coworkers started complaining, and I got pulled into the manager's office for a talking to. I didn't care; I continued to knit. I desperately needed to knit. It was the only place of solace I could find to help me to cope with everything that was going on in my life. It wasn't just about me— my children were also in a tailspin. Their father got married, and he didn't tell them until after the fact! The whole situation was a complete mess. Knitting was something I needed to help me slow down my thoughts.

The season changed and I got tired of making hats and mittens. It was time to try something new. I needed to take on something challenging! I decided to make a sweater. While looking for knitting patterns online, I found a knitting group. I was so desperate for community and friends, that I latched onto the group. I avidly read all of the blog posts and started to feel like I knew these women. Immediately when the group moderator started talking about a knit-along sweater project, I was all in. A knit-along sweater project is when a group leader chooses a project, and all the members of the group agree to knit that project along with them. The instructions can be given all at once, or in periodic increments. The leader of this group chose the pattern. Because she was going to knit it using red yarn, she called it "The Red Hot Tomato." It was the challenge that I needed.

The precious thing about any kind of piecework is that it commands your attention. You have to slow down and consider your next steps. No matter what you do, you have no choice but to take life one stitch at a time. My processes sounded like: one stitch, (don't cry), one stitch (you will live), one stitch (just breathe), one stitch (you will live), one stitch… It was in those moments of slowed thinking that I was able to start to process what was happening with my life. In those moments, all I could see was the loss, and I wasn't quite sure how I had ended up in this difficult space. I could not fully comprehend that I was in the throes of great shaking. The dead things in my life were being shaken off, and Father God was doing the work of moving me closer to Him through the use of this knitting project.

Because I had always considered myself to be an introvert, I didn't fully comprehend how desperately I craved being part of a "tribe." Attending my church had become very painful for me. Everywhere I looked my ex-husband and his new wife were being celebrated. Going to my church filled me with great anxiety. I was like a trauma victim needing immediate medical attention, but I would never allow myself to go past the hospital parking lot. I was bleeding to death, and in need of a full medical team, but my church was not equipped at that moment to help me. I needed an infusion of love and acceptance. At the time, I wanted a genuine expression of the Agape love of God. Unfortunately, I was expecting to receive it from the very human beings I had surrounded myself with. My pain was so misunderstood. Because I had not developed many genuine relationships, there were only a precious few people who knew my history with this marriage. Only a small number of people could understand the depth of my feelings of betrayal. I concluded that I had been jilted and tossed aside by my church family, just as I had been by my ex-husband. My church was no longer a place where I felt safe and loved. The stronghold of rejection was affecting my ability to see clearly. I believed I had been forsaken by the leadership and those members of the congregation that I thought were friends. Looking back, I can see how the snare of deception and defense was coiling itself around me. I was like the slow-running gazelle that the lions follow, encircle, and finally separate from the herd. I was a prime candidate for destruction because of the stronghold of rejection.

I see now how the stronghold of rejection had been constructed and was being reinforced by me feeling like my church family did not support me. Because my ability to reason was being guided by rejection, for the first time in my adult life, I was beginning to doubt God's heart and intentions toward me. Doubt comes with feelings of uncertainty. The doubt made me question or second-guess God's love for me. Doubt had come, and instead of recognizing it for what it was, a trap, I instead allowed it to open a pathway for the liar, accuser, and deceiver to speak to me. The strongholds of rejection and doubt governed my decision-making process at the time. In the garden, we first see the consequences of allowing doubt to speak to us.

Genesis 3:1-5 (NIV) states, "Now the serpent was more crafty than any of the wild animals the Lord God had made. He said to the woman, "Did God really say, 'You must not eat from any tree in the garden'?"

2 The woman said to the serpent, "We may eat fruit from the trees in the garden, 3 but God did say, 'You must not eat fruit from the tree that is in the middle of the garden, and you must not touch it, or you will die.'"

4 "You will not certainly die," the serpent said to the woman. 5 "For God knows that when you eat from it your eyes will be opened, and you will be like God, knowing good and evil."

Our enemy, the devil, has no new motives. He still lives only to steal, kill and destroy. He also has no new tactics. The lust of the flesh, the lust of the eyes, and the pride of life are all that he has in his toolbox. If we do an honest assessment, we also learn that his attacks are not about us; the object of his rage is The Most High. We are simply the weapon that he uses in his attempts to battle with God the Father. He uses these tactics to draw us away and to disparage our understanding of God. He speaks lies to birth doubt in God's intentions toward us to entice us away from the Father.

When doubt enters the mind of a believer, a crossroad is created. Do we allow doubt to linger and consider the veracity of the lie, or do we use the opportunity to affirm what we know about God's Word and move on? Lingering in doubt gives the enemy space to affirm the lie by presenting other circumstantial evidence. If we are not mindful of his tactics and schemes, we will believe the lies and live our lives based on the lies. That partnership starts to affect our mindset and perspective about the issue, and active doubt gives way to disobedience. Disobedience leads to separation from the source of truth, and that separation leads to sin and death, which we know to be the enemy's ultimate goal. John 10:10 (NIV) explains, "The thief comes only to steal and kill and destroy; I have come that they may have life, and have it to the full."

Doubt in the life of the believer can be likened to adultery in a marriage. It tears away at the fabric of the relationship and shakes the foundational trust that it is built upon. It destabilizes and eats away at the structure of the bond. We must not allow doubt to linger. If we do not deal with doubt, its negative effects will be compounded over time. We have to take action as soon as we recognize that we are being deceived and drawn away by doubt. When the enemy comes and tries to speak lies about the character of God, or His intentions toward us, we have to immediately take those thoughts captive. Similar to adultery, the sin is not only in the looking; the sin is most mature in the linger! Doubt opens the door to distrust. Because Eve lingered in the presence of the enemy and entertained his conversation, he was able to convince her that God did not have her best interest at heart. I have to admit that the enemy convinced me that God did not have my best interest at heart. Doubt is the enemy of faith, and for the first time, my great faith in God had been shaken.

WISDOM GAINED

All of us at some point will come up against the spirit of doubt that would try and shake our faith in what we know about God. Jesus had this experience after 40 days of fasting in the wilderness. (Matthew 4:1-11) The enemy came to Him and attempted to tempt Him with the lust of the flesh, the lust of the eyes, and the pride of life. The wicked one tried to take Jesus off the path, but the Lord rebuffed him with the Word. All of the enemy's responses were a reiteration of what God had said. His responses to the tempter all started with, "It is written." He presented the liar with the Word of Truth and caused him to flee. This is why the study of the Word of God is so integral to success in the life of the believer. I liken studying the Word of God to constructing a safety net and a shield. I'm a Star Trek fan, and whenever the Enterprise was coming up against an enemy, the commander would say "shields up." Knowledge of the word is like that shield, and when the enemy comes to try and tell you something that isn't true, the word of faith that is embedded in you can rise and protect you. All the alarms start to go off in your mind when you hear something that doesn't correlate with the word that is in you. Spending time in the presence of God and the study of the Word gives you a revelation of the nature and character of God. When you know God intimately, it prepares you to be better able to discern a slanderous lie that doesn't align with what you know to be true about His character so you're able to reject it.

Our trust in God and His Word are the substance of the "shield of faith" referenced in Ephesians 6:16. Our trust in God and the faith that it builds is what extinguishes the fiery dart of doubt and renders it powerless. We need to strive for the Word of God to bubble up and activate faith at the appointed time to protect us from the father of lies. Not developing a lifestyle of reading about the nature of God leaves us open and vulnerable to a doubt attack.

PRAYER

Father, thank You for loving me so much and for protecting me from the lies of the enemy. I declare that I trust in Your unfailing love. My heart is not troubled, and my heart rejoices in Your salvation. Father, I trust in Your timing. You open up windows of opportunity for me at the appointed time. I have no fear of the future because I know You hold each of my days in Your hand. I thank You for being ever-present with me. You never leave, never forsake; hope in You never disappoints. I can lean and depend on You.

Thank You Father for giving me a hunger for Your Word. I desire a deep hunger for the study of Your word to show myself approved and to arm me against the tricks of the enemy. Thank You, Lord, for depositing a well of Your Word deep within me so that it can bubble up whenever the lies of the enemy try and take me off the path. I submit myself to learning more about you. I submit myself to learning about Your character, attributes, and heart for me, through the study of Your Word. I thank You Father for honoring that commitment and blessing me with Your wisdom and with a greater measure of faith. I declare that You are my rock, my protector, my strong tower, and the One who saves me. You are my place of safety and my refuge. To God be the Glory! In Jesus' name, I pray. Amen.

SCRIPTURE FOR MEDITATION

Jeremiah 29:11 (NIV)

For I know the plans I have for you," declares the Lord, "plans to prosper you and not to harm you, plans to give you hope and a future.

FOUR

THE STRONGHOLD OF OFFENSE

"Offense robs us of the gift of God's grace and mercy that has been made available to carry us through any trial that we may endure."

The elation of being part of the knitting group and doing something new was invigorating. I immersed myself in every aspect of the planning for this sweater. The purpose of the knitting group was to draw in readers for the online version of the knitting magazine; therefore, the facilitator took her time creating engagement with the participants. Even though it was virtual, I was happy to be a part of a tribe. I thought I had found "my people." At the same time, I started shopping for a new church to attend since I no longer felt welcome at my former church home.

As I previously stated, the sweater pattern was called, The Red Hot Tomato. It was a square-necked, short sleeve sweater and the bottom hem was designed to lie at waist level. The person that I am today understands full well that a waist-level hem is not designed for this body! Because the thirst for association was so intense, I ignored the inner voice that let me know this design was not for my body type.

The young lady leading the knit-along seemed to be very likable. She reminded me of the women that I had casual conversations with at my local knitting shop, as I walked through the aisles petting the yarn and dreaming of what project would be next. She seemed like someone that I would love to have a cup of tea with and discuss topics such as the intricacies of toe-up sock knitting, how not to drop stitches, or how not to lose track of the stitch count while crafting lace. She was kind and engaging, but that was where our similarities seemingly ended. As I reflect on the sweater pattern, I realized that it did not reflect my style at all! I don't believe I would have chosen it for myself. It was plain, with a folksy design, and I wouldn't find it appealing under ideal circumstances. Again, I went with it because I so desperately wanted to be a part of something, anything! Nonetheless, I carried on like she was my best friend!

At the same time, I started attending a well-established church in our area that I knew preached sound doctrine and was true to the Word of God. My behavior was enigmatic even to myself. I sat in the back and would leave right after service. I never introduced myself to anyone; I made sure to avoid people that I knew socially. I never went up for an altar call, didn't ask for prayer, or otherwise engage with the community that I supposedly was so in need of. I didn't fit in, and I didn't love it, but I continued to go anyway. The dichotomy of my thoughts and actions was ridiculous at best and was being demonstrated in other areas of my life as well. I acted like I was so excited about knitting this sweater, but I was less than enraptured by the pattern. If anyone asked me, the church I was now attending was great, but I hadn't had more than the most superficial type of conversation with anyone in the congregation. I was miserable, fake, and a liar.

The enemy of my soul was restraining me in a stronghold of isolation and fear. Strongholds are prisons of the mind. The enemy comes and speaks a lie into your atmosphere, and if you have not fully believed what God's Word says about that thing, you will come into agreement with a lie. That lie becomes the foundation for a mindset, and spiritual bondage is built on that foundation. Lies can build strongholds of bondage in our lives because they keep us from the truth of our true identity in Christ. Isaiah 5:13 (NKJV) states, "Therefore my people have gone into captivity, because they have no knowledge." Hosea 4:6 (NKJV) conveys, "My people are destroyed for lack of knowledge." I was in a battle against rejection, loneliness, separation, and abandonment. Unfortunately, I was trying to fight alone and with human weaponry. The enemy was trying to kill my spirit and my body, and I was balled up in a corner of the ring weeping. Not having an encompassing understanding of God's love for me had allowed the idols that I erected throughout my life to take His place as my source of peace and security. Fear of abandonment had become more impactful to me than the fear of the Lord. I had become like the double-minded man mentioned in the bible; I was unstable in all of my ways.

I understand now that I was operating under the influence of a stronghold of offense. I had been hurt and disappointed by the people that I trusted most in my life. This caused a wound to develop in my soul. It affected my thoughts, feelings, and actions. The stronghold of offense disabled me from being able to move forward. I was spiritually stuck in that place of pain.

In Psalm 55:12-14 (NKJV) David laments, "For it is not an enemy who reproaches me; then I could bear it. Nor is it one who hates me who has exalted himself against me; then I could hide from him. But it was you, a man my equal, my companion, and my acquaintance. We took sweet counsel together and walked to the house of the Lord in the throng."

I was ensnared in the baited trap of offense. The undealt with offense in my heart was stunting my progress both spiritually and emotionally. I was running around seeking wisdom and encouragement from sources that did not know my heart or understand my perspective. I was trying to form relationships and bonds with people and places that God did not ordain for my life at that time. I was trying to find affirmation of my worth in people who couldn't see me. I was so disconnected from the source of my strength, that I was like a foundationless tumbleweed, being tossed around, to and fro. The devil was mopping the floor with me, and it was apparent in everything I said and did.

WISDOM GAINED

Once you recognize you are battling a spirit of offense, you begin to see it everywhere. You can see how an initial offense and the corresponding absence of repentance and forgiveness are at the root of almost every conflict. We even see it in movies! In Disney's The Lion King, Scar's jealousy of Mufasa and his offense of being usurped of succession by Simba drove him to murder his brother. The age-old account of Cain and Abel has offense at its core. Cain was offended by God for not accepting his offering, and a bitter root of jealousy was planted in his heart. The offense grew until ultimately, he murdered his brother. If you do a deep dive into any conflict, you will often find offense at the root. We often associate offense with anger and rage, but I have come to understand that offense is more often born out of devastating pain. We find ourselves unable to reconcile an unexpected action with what we believed we understood about the relationship, and the seed of offense is germinated. Unreconciled offense opens the door to pride. After that, pride comes along and waters that germinated seed. It causes us to lie to ourselves about the condition of our hearts. We start to lie to ourselves and say: "I'm not hurt. I'm okay. Who are they to hurt me? I don't care what they think or do!" Pride will tie you up and keep you from quickly repenting, and that leads to the hardening of the heart. Remember, pride is what led to satan being thrown out of heaven. We have to learn to hate pride with a perfect hatred and cast it down whenever it rises against us.

Proverbs 18:19 (NKJV) explains, "A brother offended is harder to win than a strong city, and contentions are like the bars of a castle." In biblical times, cities that were fortified were surrounded by walls. These walls were built to keep out all but those who were carefully screened for admission. If you were not a citizen in good standing, you could not enter the city. If you were from another region, you had to be able to demonstrate that you had a legitimate purpose, or you were denied entry. The infirmed were also often denied entry under the guise of public health. It is the same with us. When we are offended, we begin to construct walls around our lives, and we perform an emotional sifting of those around us. We start to look with a critical eye upon anyone trying to enter into a relationship with us. We begin to question: Why do you want to know me? What is it you are trying to gain from being in a relationship with me? We only allow in people we deem to be safe. These are the people that we don't believe have the power to hurt us. We build the walls high and wide to safeguard our hearts from suffering the pain of betrayal and misunderstanding once again. Here's another crazy piece—we often are attracted to people who have been offended by the same thing as us! We consider them to be safe because they are on our side. They understand our hurt; they empathize with our view of the world. They don't challenge our mindset because they too are caught in the same baited trap of offense. Birds of a feather flocking together proves to be detrimental in this situation.

This is no way to live. It's been said that unforgiveness is like drinking poison and expecting someone else to die. It causes a bitter root to spring up in our lives, tainting our thoughts and our actions towards others. Unaddressed offense follows the same type of demonic progression. It causes us to only look inward; it creates tunnel vision that only allows us to see our pain and our assessment of risk. We lose the ability to love unconditionally because loving unconditionally is emotionally dangerous to us.

The reality is that people will hurt you. People will disappoint you. People will let you down. It's innate in being human —we sometimes fail. The spirit of offense and the walls it constructs will protect you, but not in the way you expect. They protect you from being known. They protect you from experiencing genuine relationships. They protect you from the burden of loving people through their hard times and being loved in return. At the end of the day, is the price of offense commensurate with the return on your investment? Offense drives us to self-sufficiency and causes us to lean to our understanding. Offense robs us of the gift of God's grace and mercy that has been made available to carry us through any trial that we may endure. Offenses will come, according to scripture. It's up to you to decide whether or not you will take offense or cast it back upon the one who cares for you. The trick of the enemy in offense is that the walls that we built to protect us ultimately construct a prison designed to hold us hostage.

PRAYER

Father, You warn me in Your Word that offenses will come, and You give me instruction on how to handle them. You cautioned that if my brother sins, I should solemnly warn him, and if he earnestly repents, I should forgive him, up to seventy times seven times. You call on me to give up resentment and consider the matter settled. This is a hard word. Pain often leads me to lash out or seek my own recompense. If it was not for Your grace, Father, I would be undone. I will choose Your will and Your way when faced with pain and disappointment. I will not allow pride to drive me to take offense against my brother or sister. The enemy will not lure me into that trap. I refuse to allow my heart to be held captive by unforgiveness and resentment. Help me to see my own heart condition. Keep me from taking on a distorted understanding of others' intentions for and toward me. Help me to uncover any hidden offenses holding me hostage and stagnating my growth. I repent for agreeing with deception and disappointment and building a wall of offense around my life. I choose to examine myself much more closely than I examine others. Removing the log of offense from my own eye is my priority. I submit myself to Your corrections. Give me Your heart Father! I desire to live a life that draws others to You. May the water that flows from me be refreshing and sweet and not stink from the stagnation created by resentment. In Jesus' name, I pray. Amen.

SCRIPTURE FOR MEDITATION

Luke 17:1-4 (NKJV)

Then He said to the disciples, "It is impossible that no offenses should come, but woe to him through whom they do come! 2 It would be better for him if a millstone were hung around his neck, and he were thrown into the sea, than that he should offend one of these little ones. 3 Take heed to yourselves. If your brother sins against you, rebuke him; and if he repents, forgive him. 4 And if he sins against you seven times in a day, and seven times in a day returns to you, saying, 'I repent,' you shall forgive him."

FIVE

THE STRONGHOLDS OF FEAR AND PEOPLE PLEASING

"You can live a life devoid of the damaging effects of fear, but that requires stepping out on faith and trusting the vision that God has given you for your life."

Now that I had committed to being in the knit-a-long, it was time to purchase the yarn. I went to my local yarn shop looking for the yarn specified by the pattern instruction. When I got there, they only had one color of that specific yarn—light blue. I had envisioned the sweater being a shade of red like the group leader, or at least a hot pink or fuchsia. I would have even settled for a shade of purple, but they only had light blue. I asked the shop owner if she could order the yarn for me in a different shade, but she stated that it would take a couple of weeks for it to arrive. The price tag was also quite a shock. The amount of yarn that I would need would cost me $90 which at the time, was quite an investment.

The knit-a-long was about to start! I panicked, and anxiety overtook me. I had to join in with the other ladies on time! I caved and purchased the expensive light blue yarn that I didn't like and that I couldn't afford. This was textbook approval-seeking behavior, and I now realize I was operating in the spirits of inferiority and people-pleasing that had plagued me throughout my life.

People-pleasing at a young age forced me to give up on the dreams that I had in my heart. When I was a teenager, I remember thinking that I would like to be an English professor or a writer. As I stated previously, I had a deep love for books, and I was drawn to anything that had to do with writing. I had a collection of journals, diaries, and colorful writing utensils. Those things are still a passion of mine to this day. My mother gifted me with a typewriter during my junior year in high school, and I had visions of using it to write novels like the Jessica Fletcher character in the television series Murder She Wrote. I could definitely see myself living the life of an author and professor one day.

When I discussed my career plans with my parents, I was told that I needed to be more practical. There was no college fund set aside for me. I did well with my schoolwork, so the hope was that I would earn scholarships. My father was clear— I needed to choose something that would give me a marketable skill and wouldn't require several years of schooling. That year the asthmatic condition that I suffered from intensified, and I needed to meet a respiratory therapist at the local hospital. Several other coincidences aligned, and I gave up my dream of becoming an English professor and pursued a career in respiratory therapy. At the time, I could train for two years and then begin to work, so it checked all of the boxes my father had laid out for me. I wasn't brave enough to go against my father's wishes. My mother had gone to school and became a nurse. She agreed that becoming a respiratory therapist was a good path, so I wasn't able to build an alliance there either. As I had done for all of my life, I put on a good face and convinced myself that it was what I wanted. Fear convinced me that pursuing writing, theater, and music were too whimsical for someone like me. I was too afraid to take the risk. The strongholds of people-pleasing and fear taught me that I needed to follow a path that led to an outcome that I could measure and control.

I went to school, earned my RT degree, and began my career. It has been good to me over the years, but I often look back with regret on not having pursued my heart's desire until now, so many years later. My parents did the best that they could with the knowledge they had. I realized that they were the product of growing up in the depression era. They were not risk-tolerant because in their eyes risk-taking could be deadly. My parents needed to know that I would be able to care for myself, and a healthcare career was what they considered to be safe. I adopted that mindset, and walked in those narrow boundaries, never realizing that my partnership with the spirit of fear was building a self-limiting prison.

I am still working to understand all of the factors that contributed to my evolution into being an approval-seeking, people-pleaser. Most likely it developed out of the conglomeration of all of my life experiences. Because it went unrecognized for the malignancy that it was, and grew unchecked, it intensified in its effect. My lack of self-belief, and my ignorance of who and whose I am caused me to intently seek validation outside of God and His Word.

The season where my marriage ended is where my need for approval showed up in many ways. I was seeking approval when I was not honest with myself about not being fond of the design of the sweater. People-pleasing showed up when I did not acknowledge that its design was not a match for my body type. Also, spending $90 on yarn that wasn't even a color that I liked just so I could feel a part of a community of strangers was a sign of trying to seek approval. In addition, I showed that I did not value myself by allowing my ex-husband to flaunt his girlfriends in my face and disrespect me in other ways while choosing to bear it in silence. Furthermore, I chose not to call out racist behaviors in my workplace that were hurtful and derogatory to avoid conflict and be accepted. All of it was and is fruit from the same demonic tree. I did not stand up and demand that I be treated better because deep within myself, I did not believe that I deserved better.

WISDOM GAINED

Discerning that you are operating in a spirit of fear and people-pleasing can be tricky because it can come in so many forms. First, fear is one of the oldest tricks of the enemy. Fear drove Adam and Eve to hide when they heard the voice of God instead of coming to commune with Him as they had before. We learn from scripture that God has not given us a spirit of fear, neither is it what He has ordained for our lives. Therefore, since it is not of or from Him, we have authority over it. You can live a life devoid of the damaging effects of fear, but that requires stepping out on faith and trusting the vision that God has given you for your life.

The desire to be loved and accepted is natural. Because God is love, and we are made in His image, giving love and desiring to be loved are ingrained qualities of His creation. As with all ideas, the enemy likes to take noble desires and pervert them. He speaks falsehoods that produce fear and rejection in our hearts. We start to hear: "You are not loveable. You are not desirable. You don't have friends because no one deems you worthy to befriend. People don't like you; they are just using your gifts and talents for their gain. You should change who you are—maybe then you will be accepted. You are damaged. You are ugly." Lie after lie, until your defenses fail, and you succumb to the image the enemy has created for you. Individuals who have not been taught who they are in Christ can easily fall prey to the damage of these lies. That person begins to contort themselves to fit into a mold of someone else's making. Fear of rejection causes them to shrink back and not share their authentic selves with those around them. In time, they are so diminished, that the world loses the gift of them that God designed from the foundations of the earth.

As humans, we fear the unknown. We want the path to be laid out before us, so we can evaluate it. We want to know where all the pitfalls are, identify all of the high and low places, and be able to see the final destination. We do this so that we can determine whether or not we want to pursue a thing or not. All of us want the ability to decide whether the sacrifice necessary is worth it to us. In other words, we lack trust in God.

When I was young, my dad would sometimes ask me and my sisters to go take a ride with him. Even if we asked, he wouldn't always tell us where we were going. He'd say, "Just come take a ride with me." My younger sisters would often choose to stay home, but I would go most of the time. Sometimes we would end up in some obscure junkyard where he was looking to purchase a random car part. Other times, we would end up going shopping or out to eat. One time, in particular, I came back with a beautiful new coat and leather boots. I also had handfuls of candy to share with my sisters. Regardless of where we ended up, I enjoyed going on the ride with my dad. He wasn't a man of many words, but we would drive and listen to music, and spend time together. I trusted that wherever he was taking me, it would work out in my favor.

Our Father God asks us to trust Him in the way that He is taking us. He asks us to simply come along for the ride, and know that He is a good, good Father. Isn't He greater than our earthly fathers? If our earthly father is able and willing to give good gifts, how much more can we expect from our heavenly Father that knows all of our flaws, and yet loves us unconditionally. To move forward, we have to both recognize and acknowledge that we are operating in a spirit of fear. Once we do that, we can renounce it, and come out of partnership with it. Psalm 55:22 (NIV) says, "Cast your cares on the Lord and he will sustain you; he will never let the righteous be shaken." God is a firm foundation. We can place the full weight of our hopes and fears on Him, knowing that there is no shifting in Him.

The God of the universe declares that He loves us unconditionally. He knows our faults and our failings, and yet, He loves us just the same. There is no shadow of turning in Him; He will not change His mind about you. His great love extended itself to the giving of His only begotten Son to die for the remission of our sins. He was faultless but found us worthy of Him even enduring death on a cross. Also, here is the kicker— even if there had only been one of us requiring redemption through His blood sacrifice, He would have done it just the same. He is the one that leaves the 99 to save the one little lost sheep. What kind of love is this? Who are we to belittle His sacrifice? When we walk in agreement with the devil who says we are unworthy of love, we make the Father out to be a liar. Commit to doing the work of deliverance or wanting to be set free from negative thinking patterns so that you can accept the gift of love that has been bought for you.

PRAYER

Father, I come before You today and cast all of my cares, fears, and anxieties on You because I know that You love and care for me. I declare that

You are my Good Shepherd and that I can trust Your lead. I decree and declare that I am anxious for nothing. The weight of fear and anxiety is not mine to carry, for You have said that Your yoke is easy, and Your burden is light. As an act of my will, I stand on the Word of God and walk in supernatural faith. Your peace stands guard over my heart and mind, and I know that You will keep me safe.

Father, I acknowledge You as my keeper. Your Word says in Isaiah 26:3 that You will keep my mind in perfect peace because I take hold of Your truth and trust in You. I come before You and lay down all my defenses. I stand naked and vulnerable before You. I choose to embrace Your rest.

Father, I declare that I am strong and courageous; I do not embrace fear, as You have not given it to me. (2 Timothy 1:7) I will not bow to it or partner with it. You are the stronghold of my life! You love me with relentless love! I am never alone because You promise to be with me wherever I go. I will move forward with confidence, knowing that You are the God of angel armies! I am victorious in everything I do because You, the Lord, will fight my battles.

My heart greatly praises You, my Defender! Thank You Father for Your mercy and grace that are new every morning. I bless and exalt Your name! In Jesus' name, I pray. Amen!

SCRIPTURE FOR MEDITATION

Galatians 1:10 (NIV)

10 Am I now trying to win the approval of human beings, or of God? Or am I trying to please people? If I were still trying to please people, I would not be a servant of Christ.

SIX

THE STRONGHOLD OF REJECTION

"Freedom comes by asking the Holy Spirit to expose the open door that has given room for this spirit to operate in our life."

I brought my expensive blue yarn home and began the knit-a-long on time with all the other ladies. I found my flow and was keeping up the pace. During the process, the leader realized that she would need to modify the pattern to better accommodate her body shape. Specifically, she mentioned knitting in darts around the bust area. She used a couple of blog posts to explain the process of how we could increase stitches in one area and decrease in another area to make the accommodation. She explained the general process but could not give each knitter explicit instructions because the modification was specific to our body measurements. I panicked once again! This wasn't written into the pattern! There was no set guide for me to follow! What was I supposed to do? It was my first time encountering this type of free-form guidance, and I was lost. The whole thing was too much for me to grasp. I was also at a place in the pattern where I would have to go back and undo stitches, and I was afraid to do that. I thought: What if I lost my place? What if I couldn't get back on track? Undoing, or ripping back, as it is called, was scary to me. I wasn't sure I could successfully do it; consequently, I chose to continue without making the suggested modifications. I never said I didn't believe it was necessary or that I thought it wouldn't be beneficial— I said I was afraid to do it. In fact, I knew full well that my ample bust line needed the accommodation that adding darts would have provided, but fear of failure held me back. I continued to work fanatically on the sweater. I neglected other duties and responsibilities to knit. It took unnatural precedence over my life. There was even a day that I found myself hiding in the bathroom at my job to work on the sweater. It had evolved into a golden calf before my eyes.

Working on this sweater meant that I got to ignore what was in front of me regarding my divorce. I did not want to deal with the pain that my marriage and divorce brought in my life. I was legally divorced on paper, but in my heart, the connection remained. My devotion to a man that obviously no longer loved me was pathetic and sad. I remember one occasion specifically when we happened to be together. He said to me, "You need to let me go. When you touch me, I can feel you not letting go." He was doing his best to warn me and create the needed distance between us, but I chose to ignore what was right in my face. I know now that this was idolatry and an ungodly soul-tie that had me in bondage. At the time, I was unable to release either of us from the relationship.

I had an unnatural fanaticism over my ex-husband that had exhibited itself throughout the life of the relationship. While we were still married, his mother died, and his girlfriend came to the funeral. We were seated in the service, and his girlfriend, who was seated behind me, reached over me to give him a comforting touch on his shoulder. I was humiliated and angry and should have gotten up and left. Instead, I just bowed my head in shame. My father, who witnessed this, was so angry with me, he could have spit! I remember him telling me that I better not ever again allow myself to be treated like that! If only I heeded his advice. There were many displays of my partnership and agreement with a spirit of rejection over the years. So many red flags, so many indications of what was true and what was false, so many opportunities to make the necessary modifications and improve my situation, but the strongholds of fear and abandonment continued to have their way.

WISDOM GAINED

The spirit of rejection is an oppressive spirit that attacks the part of you that desires love, acceptance, and affirmation. It lies about how God feels about you, and partners with the orphan spirit to make you feel worthless. The orphan spirit makes you feel as if you do not have a good Father in heaven that loves you. The opposite of having an orphan spirit is understanding that we are children of God. Rejection partnered with an orphan spirit can manifest itself as self-reliance and insecurity. In addition, rejection and having an orphan mindset drives people to seek out praise, approval, and acceptance from man. The affected being has an inordinate need for personal achievement and recognition to impress God and others. They link duty and work against God's favor, and they are often plagued with shame and guilt as they compare themselves to others.

Rejection has to be cast out, but for it to no longer take root in your mind, it has to be displaced and put to death by a shifting of the mind to understand that God sees us as sons, not slaves. To have victory over feeling rejected means we have to fully accept God's love and the grace He extends to us. In my case, operating from the mindset of rejection had been developing over a lifetime.

Freedom comes by asking Holy Spirit to expose the open door that has given room for this spirit to operate in our life. Once we understand what mindsets have given rejection space in our daily life, we will need to repent for agreeing with the lies that rejection and the orphan spirit have spoken over our lives. Take every errant thought captive and bring it into submission to the Lord Jesus Christ. Diligently study and meditate on the Word daily, declaring God's love over the lies of the enemy. Whom the Son makes free is free indeed. We do not have to remain in bondage to rejection. Our Father is standing at the doorway waiting for us, His son or daughter, to return to His love.

PRAYER

Father, I confess that I have partnered with rejection which has led me to think like an orphan in Your Kingdom. I believed the lies of the enemy that said that I am not worthy to be called Your son/daughter. I have partnered with rejection and tried to make myself worthy through works and sacrifices. I repent for living life in this manner. I understand now that You value relationship over sacrifice. You value a broken spirit and contrite heart You will not despise.

Father, I renounce all agreement with rejection and the orphan spirit. I am not an orphan! You have declared me to be a joint-heir with Christ! You have seated me in heavenly places. My righteousness is not determined by anything that I can do on my own. My righteousness was conferred upon me by the sacrifice of the Lord Jesus Christ. I cannot purchase it! It is a gift from You. Strengthen me to fully apprehend Your love for me. Help me to clear away all of the errors that have clouded my vision and led me away from Your intentions for me. I desire to be in the center of Your will. In Jesus' name, I pray. Amen.

SCRIPTURE FOR MEDITATION

Ephesians 2:8-9 (NKJV)

8 For by grace you have been saved through faith, and that not of yourselves; it is the gift of God, 9 not of works, lest anyone should boast.

SEVEN

THE STRONGHOLD OF SHAME

"Hidden, untreated wounds don't heal well."

My diligent attention to knitting paid off, and finally, the sweater was completed. I was so proud of it! The stitches were so neat and even. It was structurally perfect. I took my time with all the finishing steps, cutting away any loose strings, and wet blocking it (which is done to make sure it is shaped per your specifications). I set the sweater aside to dry and waited with anticipation for the day when I would be able to try on the finished product. That day finally arrived, and I unpinned it from the blocking board and slipped it over my head. I looked in the mirror, and….it looked terrible. I mean really terrible! I immediately knew that I should have taken the time to knit in those bust darts! The large gauge cotton yarn had knit up into a bulky fabric, which added unnecessary (and uncomplimentary) girth to my upper body. It was ill-fitting, frumpy, and unshapely. I was crushed!

I often heard the saying, "the weight of disappointment," but I didn't fully understand what it meant until that moment. The crushing weight of the illusions I had built fell on me; the tower of delusion about the sweater and the deceptions I had built around my life and identity became intermingled and fell in a heap of broken stone all around me. It was the last straw; I couldn't go any further. At that moment I understood what the sweater had represented to me. I was trying to knit my existence together with yarn I didn't like, and into a pattern, I didn't care for. I was grasping for something to hold on to because I felt myself free-falling into an abyss of grief, regret, unforgiveness, and offense. The safety net that I tried to create for myself was full of gaping holes. I didn't know myself anymore. I remember calling my mom and weeping. "He left me, Mommy! I'm so hurt!" She was silent on the other end of the phone, and just allowed me to weep. She said, "Don't cry; you're gonna be alright. Just hold on." That is all I was doing. At the time, I was holding on to a thread. I once read a book about a woman who had suffered a great loss; I believe she had tragically lost her mother. I can't recall the title, but the sentence she used to describe her agony stayed with me. She said, "I was cut so deeply that I felt that I would limp for the rest of my life." I considered calling the crisis hotline, but instead, I called my friend, Leslie. She talked to me until I could breathe again.

My friends and co-workers all knew that I had been working on the sweater, so eventually, people started to ask me about it. I was too embarrassed to tell them that it was an utter failure, so I would just say, "Yep! I finished it!" People asked to see it, but I made lame excuses and put them off. I couldn't stand to look at it. The sweater was a reminder of everything about my life that was ill-fitting, poorly designed, and uncomplimentary. The sweater that I thought that I would love had disappointed me, and I hated the sight of it. A decision had to be made, so the conversation with myself began. "Give it away?" No. It was too valuable both monetarily and emotionally. "Wear it anyway?" No, I wasn't confident enough to do that, and I was too proud to admit that something I had created was unflattering. "Set it aside, and don't deal with it? Yep, that works for me!" At first, I felt like it did work. I adopted avoidance as a strategy to mask my pain.

I fell into a place of numbness. On the surface, I appeared functional and fine, but grief was always lingering at the borders of my mind and could overtake me at any moment. I cried every day. I cried in my car; I cried in my bed at night. I even cried in the bathroom at work. Heaviness fell on me like a wet wool cloak, smothering me. I watched my children grieve and begin to spiral downward, and my heart hurt even more. I felt responsible for their pain because I had not faced my reality. I felt as if I created an atmosphere that allowed them to be hurt and disappointed. The environment that I allowed for my children nurtured their offenses, some of which remain to this day. I was emotionally injured. Trying to exist was an overwhelming task. Hidden, untreated wounds don't heal well. I felt like God had fully abandoned me, and I was angry. Shame had me believing that everyone I knew could see what an emotional wreck I was. I'm sure those close to me knew I was suffering, but shame made me see scorn and ridicule in every setting I went in. I just knew everyone could see what a mess I was and were pitying me. The anguish caused me to become reclusive. I only did what I had to do; I couldn't even go to church. I was taking a full out thrashing from the enemy, and I felt helpless to prevent it.

WISDOM GAINED

After Adam and Eve sinned and ate of the forbidden fruit, Genesis 3:7 (NIV) says, "Then the eyes of both of them were opened, and they realized they were naked; so they sewed fig leaves together and made coverings for themselves." Through Adam and Eve's disobedience, shame entered the earth. We learn from this scripture and our own lives that shame has a magnifying effect. It magnifies our emotions and our self-importance. It causes us to attribute qualities to others that they may or may not be exhibiting.

The stronghold of shame enabled me not to seek out the help that I desperately needed. Shame led me to exhibit prideful behaviors. I fell into the trap of thinking that God owed me something. My mind wandered thinking: I was a faithful servant, nothing abysmal was supposed to happen to me. I kept asking: Why didn't God fix this situation for me? When we do not deal with shame, we have the opportunity to think about God, people, and ourselves in a distorted way.

Shame did not allow me to grow in intimacy with God. His highest desire is for us to have a relationship with Him. My shame and sense of self-entitlement continued to put a chasm between my Father and myself. We have to decide today to be healed from shame so that we can accurately see God as our good and loving Father. Understanding God's nature helps us to find out our true identity as well. Furthermore, once we have an accurate view of God, we can embrace the people who He sends to help us.

PRAYER

Father, I acknowledge that I have been battling a spirit of shame; I have allowed it to speak inferiority, unworthiness, and insecurity into my heart and soul. Please forgive me for trying to find affirmation in sources outside of You. I confess that I have valued the approval of others more than I have valued a relationship with You. I repent for resorting to isolation when I felt ashamed instead of calling on You, the source of my strength. When I feel like hiding, please strengthen me to seek out those who will speak life and that more abundantly into my spirit.

Please forgive me for shrinking and contorting myself to conform to the specifications of others outside of You. I choose to believe that I am who You say that I am—beloved, accepted, forgiven, righteous, fearfully, and wonderfully made. Your grace is sufficient for me; Your power is made perfect in my weakness. I am so grateful that You love and care for me.

In Jesus' name, I pray. Amen

SCRIPTURE FOR MEDITATION

Psalm 103:8-14 (NKJV)

8 The Lord is merciful and gracious,
Slow to anger, and abounding in mercy.
9 He will not always strive with us,
Nor will He keep His anger forever.
10 He has not dealt with us according to our sins,
Nor punished us according to our iniquities.
11 For as the heavens are high above the earth,
So great is His mercy toward those who fear Him;
12 As far as the east is from the west,
So far has He removed our transgressions from us.
13 As a father pities his children,
So the Lord pities those who fear Him.
14 For He knows our frame;
He remembers that we are dust.

EIGHT

THE PLACE OF CONFRONTATION

Psalm 34:18 (NKJV)

The Lord is near to those who have a broken heart, And saves such as have a contrite spirit.

There is a day that I believe I will never forget for the rest of my life. It was Valentine's Day, and my son asked me to stop at the market on the way to drop him off for school. He wanted to buy some little girl a box of candy and a teddy bear. I waited in the car, and as was my usual, I started to cry. On this particular morning, I lamented to God over all that I had done and all that I had lost. I even let God know I felt that He had mistreated me. I cried out to Him about everything I had tolerated and the price that I paid to stay in this relationship. I told Him that one of the reasons I had done all of this was in my efforts to try and honor Him and the covenant I made. The tears were flowing hot and bitter down my face, dripping onto my coat and the steering wheel of the car. Then, it happened—I heard the voice of God speak in my spirit. He said, "I didn't ask you to do any of that." That simple declaration was like a bucket of ice-cold water being thrown in my face! It shocked me, and I instantly became angry! Before I knew it, presumption rose in me. I found myself trying to confront the God of the universe. I spoke through clenched teeth and said, "What did you say to me?" The reply was a repeat of what He already said. He repeated to me, "I didn't ask you to do any of that." I was speechless. My son soon returned to the car, so I gathered my emotions, but I couldn't wait to get back home to address what I heard in my spirit.

I finally ran up against the only being willing and able to check me on my nonsense, the One and Only Living God. Hearing the words, "I didn't ask you to do any of that" was the place of my breaking. I thought I had been walking in brokenness before that moment, but I wasn't. I was walking in self-pity, regret, condemnation, and shame, but it was not brokenness. A broken and contrite heart was what He desired from me, but bitterness and gall were all that I had to offer God.

That moment that I heard God challenge my thoughts created a hard stop for me. I liken it to being in a car and hitting a huge pothole. The kind of pothole that makes our cars bounce and the bang of the impact of the vehicle with the road makes our teeth chatter. As soon as we get a chance, we pull off the road, hop out and walk around the car inspecting it for damage. That day, I hit a major pothole. It forced me to step out of my situation and do some introspective work. I needed to assess the extent of the damage.

I did a recap, of sorts, of everything that had happened to me over the past several years. My ex-husband had remarried, which had come as a total surprise to me because I believed in my heart of hearts that we would reconcile. That proved to be a painful miscalculation, and it had thrown me into an emotional and physical tailspin. I had three children that I had to continue to care for, so I needed to get myself together. I felt betrayed by my ex-husband, but more acutely, I felt betrayed by God. That was the introspection that I needed to be honest about. I felt betrayed by God. The Father that I believed loved me unconditionally had set me up to be hurt, or so I believed. When I heard Him say in my spirit, "I didn't ask you to do any of that," I was knocked for a loop. I honestly and truly believed that He had! If God did not tell me to stay in that relationship and tolerate being abused and mistreated, then how did I get here? Somehow, I allowed myself to be disconnected from my source of truth. That disconnection diverted me from my right path. There was a lie somewhere that I had agreed with and internalized, and I needed to, in the vernacular of my people, "Get this lie straight!"

Anger and confusion propelled me into taking a long look in the mirror. I finally could see that I was off track, and I needed to get my bearings. I evaluated all the places I made missteps, and wrong turns. I realized that I surrendered my entire existence to the enemy. I could see that I lived in a pit of misery by my own accord. It was time to pick myself up. It was time for me to lift my head. I reviewed all the fears and concerns that had been drivers in my mad dash to nowhere special. How could this have happened? Like the prodigal son, I found myself in the hog's pen, and I had a "coming to myself" moment. My heart cried, "Father! Help me to see what I cannot see! Take the blinders off my eyes and help me to judge clearly!" Like the good Father that He is, He began the process of washing me with His Word. It was then that I was able to line up what I believed and agreed with against what the Word of God said.

The enemy told me that people were laughing at me. The wicked one informed me that I looked weak and stupid. I kept beating myself up, saying, "I thought you were smart!" The Father reminded me that in Isaiah 54:17 (NLT) it says "But in that day, no weapon turned against you will succeed. You will silence every voice raised up to accuse you. These benefits are enjoyed by the servants of the Lord; their vindication will come from me. I, The Lord, have spoken. I felt intimidation being washed away.

I was ashamed of being divorced. I believed I was a failure as a wife. The Bible states the opposite. Isaiah 54:4 says, "Fear not; you will no longer live in shame. Don't be afraid; there is no more disgrace for you. You will no longer remember the shame of your youth and the sorrows of your widowhood. For your creator will be your husband; the Lord of heaven's armies is His Name! He is your redeemer, the Holy One of Israel, the God of all the Earth. For the Lord has called you back from your grief - as though you were a young wife abandoned by her husband" (New Living Translation Bible, 2015). When I read this scripture, I felt the weight of shame being washed away.

The enemy wanted me to believe that I wouldn't be able to provide for my children in the same way. He even threatened me with losing my house! God said the opposition in Psalm 37:23-25 (NIV), "The Lord makes firm the steps of the one who delights in Him; though he may stumble, he will not fall, for the Lord upholds him with His hand. I was young and now I am old, yet I have never seen the righteous forsaken or their children begging bread." That was when I felt the burden of fear being washed away. God would help me take care of my children and show Himself as their great Father as well.

The enemy tried to leverage my isolation and fear of being left alone. He antagonized me saying, "Your children will grow up, leave you, and you will be alone." Isaiah 49:14-16 and 26 (NLT), states, "Yet Jerusalem says, "The Lord has deserted us; the Lord has forgotten us." "Never! Can a mother forget her nursing child? Can she feel no love for the child she has borne? But even if that were possible, I would not forget you! See, I have written your name in the palms of my hands. Always in my mind is a picture of Jerusalem's walls in ruin. (26) All the world will know that I, the Lord, am your savior and your redeemer, the Mighty One of Israel." Fear of abandonment rolled off of me like a river.

Eventually, I had to address the most painful lie of all. The biggest lie I believed was that God didn't care about me or my broken heart. God whispered to me through Psalm 56:8 NLT, "You keep track of all of my sorrows. You have collected all my years in your bottle. You have recorded each one in your book. My enemies will retreat when I call to you for help. This I know; God is on my side."

God is on My Side

God is on my side was the single truth from the Word of God that broke the chains of offense and unforgiveness off of my stony heart. It became more than words. It became the revelation that renewed my hope in Him. The divine truth of God's love for me was like being in a room flooded with sunlight after being in a subterranean cave. He had chosen me! I was grateful for the light, but I was also overwhelmed with emotion. I was ecstatically happy, and heartbroken at the same time. Grief and regret filled my heart. I wrongfully accused God! I allowed the enemy to malign His character and speak lies to me about His love for me, and His concern for me. I fell for the wicked one's deceptions and believed a lie. I was both embarrassed and so very sorry. I stopped and began to apologize to God. I asked for the Father's forgiveness for allowing my sorrow to call His love for me into question. I asked Him for forgiveness for questioning His motives and accusing Him of abuse and abandonment. I falsely accused Him and believed the enemy's lies not only about God but also about myself. I repented for trying to manipulate God and my ex-husband into fitting into the paradigm that I had constructed.

Jesus bore the burden of accusation that rightfully belonged to me. That is what Jesus did for all of us on the cross. I felt alone and abandoned. I lost friends and had people turn their backs on me. In my moment of deep introspection, I was reminded in Isaiah 53:3 (NKJV) that, "He was despised and rejected by men, A Man of sorrows and acquainted with grief." I cried rivers of tears, but the Word speaks of Him in the garden in Luke 22:24 NKJV, "And being in agony, He prayed more earnestly. Then His sweat became like great drops of blood falling down to the ground." All of this was done for my sake and my tears. I had been humiliated and felt ashamed, but the Word reminded me that Jesus was despised. He was humiliated for my sins. He experienced great sorrow for the sake of setting me from sin. I fell on my face and began to weep before Him. I was so very sorry for accusing Him of not truly loving me.

When I had that vulnerable moment with God, He released His mercy and His grace into the room. He continued to make it evident that He is a good Father. During that encounter, I felt His love wash over me in a way that I have been unable to describe. The word speaks of Him being close to the brokenhearted. I felt that indescribable closeness on that day. He drew near to me and began to restore my soul. I felt like a child who had been in a fit of crying. My face was hot, and my breathing was ragged. At that moment, my eyes were swollen, and I was drained. There was no more fight in me. The brokenness that leads to restoration had finally arrived. I was finally ready to embrace His healing power. I began what would be a few years of pouring my heart out to Him and receiving His correction and realignment of my mindsets and motives. A great price had been paid for my healing. It was past time for me to fully walk in it. The new season was upon me.

NINE

THE TURNING POINT

"The path to abundant life involves introspection and high levels of truth-telling."

Have you ever found yourself on the wrong side of an argument? You just knew that your position was correct. You had chosen a side and were committed to defending it come hell or high water. Then the unthinkable happens— new information is released, and then you realize that you were tricked into supporting someone or something that did not reflect your values or your mindsets. You have egg on your face, and a great big helping of humble pie has been dished up for your dining pleasure. That is the absolute worst! At that moment, you have a couple of options at your disposal. You could ignore or deny what you know to be true and stay on the original path. The other opposition is that you could admit that you were wrong, make whatever apologies are warranted, and then try to figure out exactly how you managed to be deceived. I decided to choose the latter option, and let me tell you, pride gave me a run for my money. Every time I would get to a place that required me to admit that I had believed a lie, I would try to explain my thought process. Sometimes I would also try to position the matter in a different light so that my wrong belief could be explained away. Truth and deception were battling for governance over my soul; this was difficult, painful work, but I committed to getting it done. It was the most hard-fought battle of my life, but I did not fight it alone.

I finally healed enough to return to our church fellowship via the women's life group that I was a part of. I was still uncomfortable in the sanctuary, but the life group was a place of safety for me. The women became like sisters to me, and they walked alongside me until I could regain my strength and begin to recover. After much encouragement from my natural family, my church family, and three different counselors, I was able to rise out of the pit of clinical depression. I looked around and found that there was much in my life that had fallen into disarray due to neglect. The difference was that I was not content to leave it in that condition. I decided to live.

As I began to rectify my thoughts, I also desired to clear my physical environment. My first project was to clear out the clutter I accumulated in my bedroom. It was at that time that I ran across the sweater. I was bagging up clothes to give away, and the sweater showed up in the stack. I picked it up off the pile to look it over. It was crumpled and wrinkled from having been tossed aside and forgotten. I pulled it from its hiding place amongst the other garments that had outlived their usefulness, sat down, and smoothed it over my lap. I admired the handiwork that had created it. I ran my fingers over the ribbing around the squared collar and the mitered corners. I remembered how meticulous I had been while crafting it. I had such lofty plans for this little garment. I remembered being focused on all the attention to detail, making sure that it reflected the pattern perfectly. I ran my fingers over the decorative houndstooth pattern knit over the midsection and thought about how it was the first time that I successfully used stranded knitting. I remembered my angst in trying to join in the new color without messing up the rows. I wanted it to be perfect. I inspected the cap sleeves and admired how carefully they had been executed. I also gave it a critical eye; after all, I had been perfecting my craft for a few years by now, and in my mind, I could see my missteps. A couple of darts at the bust, a little lengthening of the bodice, and it would have been much better suited for my body. I reflected on the yarn, and how the large gauge cotton was not a choice that I would have made now that I had a little more expertise on yarn fabrics. "I should have adapted the pattern and used a finer gauge yarn with a bit of stretch to it. Then, the sweater would have been better, more suitable, flattering even,"

I thought to myself. I knit many things, but this was the first thing that I had birthed and created from a place of pain. I could not leave it in this unredeemed space. I could not let it continue to exist as a representation of regret and shame. Instantly, I thought about the many hours I spent crafting each stitch. There were tears knit into this sweater. There were crushed hopes and dreams knit into this sweater. Grief and resentment had been interwoven into the fabric. It was a representation of the sufficiency of God's grace toward me. It personified how in my place of weakness, I was able to lean into God's perfect strength. It was more than a garment—it was a representation of what I had overcome.

It was decision time again. I asked myself: Should I throw it away, give it away, or set it aside again for another few years? I knew I had to keep it, but it wasn't usable in its present form. It was at that moment that I heard in my spirit, "Make it over again." "Make it over again?" I asked. "You mean unravel it and make it into something different?" "Yes, make it over again" was what I heard reiterated in my spirit.

Holy Spirit began to minister to me about the life that He intended for me. One morning, I was sitting in my backroom watching television. I think I was watching the Hallmark channel. During that time, I was admiring all the little shops and bookstores in the imaginary New England location of the movie. I started thinking about my life, and how I wished it had been different. It was a very pensive moment, but then I heard the voice in my spirit. "The life you have is the one you chose. Because I am good, I blessed your choices; however, it was not the life I intended. Do you want the life I intended?" The life He intended? What would that look like? I started thinking about what my life would look like if I could reimagine it. I dreamed about a cottage near the water; a place where I could knit and write and have a little cupcakery. A peaceful place where all of the parts of me that I had suppressed could mature into their highest potential.

At that moment, I thought about the sweater; I thought about my life. Could I make it over again? Could I go back and modify the pattern to create something new? Why couldn't I? What did I have to lose? It was at that moment that I had to make a decision. I asked myself: Are you going to trust God or not?

I took hold of that wrinkly, crumpled, unflattering sweater, turned it inside out, and found the place where I made the last stitch and tied the last knot, and then...I untied it! I tentatively began to unravel it. I held my breath as I pulled out the first few stitches and took a look at the small bit of crinkly unraveled yarn. There was still time for me to re-knit those stitches and re-tie the knot, but I exhaled and kept going. As I continued to slowly unravel the sweater, thoughts of what new thing I could create swirled around in my mind's eye.

It felt like fear was being unraveled along with all of those stitches. The more I unraveled the freer I felt. Not only was I untying the sweater, but I was also untying myself from all of the broken dreams and disappointments of my past. I was unraveling the foundational lies that had dictated my movement and my mindsets for almost 50 years. I felt brave! I felt revived! I could finally breathe, and more importantly, I finally was able to envision myself differently. It was time to reintroduce myself to the young girl that wanted to sing, write, and create for a living. The one who got squashed by the fears of others. The one who had been conditioned not to imagine a life beyond the borders pre-determined by others' expectations. It was one of the most liberating moments of my life.

WISDOM GAINED

Living a life that embodies spiritual, mental, and physical health requires that we make difficult choices. It would have been easy to paint a picture in this book that castigated my ex-husband, his family, my church family, and many others. That story would have been one-sided, unfair, and incomplete. Portraying myself as an unfortunate soul, victimized by the evil intentions of others may have engendered sympathy, and perhaps a greater audience, but it would not have produced freedom and life. The path to abundant life involves introspection and high levels of truth-telling. Having an abundant life mindset requires us to move past surface revelation and convenient neat explanations. The work of excavating the territory of one's own heart is laborious, tedious, and sometimes frightening. We will not always be pleased by the answers we uncover as we continue to ask ourselves why we are in the condition we are in, and why things are the way that they are. However, if we commit to doing the work, and commit to not turning away no matter what we see, the end result will prove to have been worth the investment. There is redemption at the end of the road.

Psalm 119:71 (NIV) says, "It was good for me to be afflicted so that I might learn your decrees." I have to be honest; I never really understood that scripture. It sounded false and sadistic. Who would say that it was good that they had endured suffering? As I stand on the other side of all the pain and struggle that I overcame, I have gained a new understanding and appreciation for what is being communicated in this verse. It was good that I was stripped of a false identity constructed by the expectations of others. It taught me how to love and appreciate my uniqueness. My journey taught me that it was good that I walked through the pain of rejection. It birthed self-love and self-acceptance into me. I found out that it was good that people in my life disappointed me. It was great that the unfair expectations that I had placed on them were exposed. It taught me how to properly assess relationships and to demand reciprocation from those that build relationships with me. It caused me to seek out deliverance and freedom from people-pleasing.

Furthermore, it was beneficial that I cried out to God in brokenheartedness. I needed to confess my disappointment and confusion about how I believed He had treated me. It was then that the lies I had believed were exposed, and I was able to reconcile my deception by the washing of the Word of God.

Throughout my healing journey, I underwent a deconstructive process. God helped me tear down the false beliefs and walls of offense that had imprisoned me for decades. I now stand on the other side, positioned to pursue abundant living. Most importantly, I gained a greater understanding of the Omnipresent God, the one who never leaves. I came to the full realization that it was not God's desire that I would be in pain. He did, however, use it for His Glory and the advancement of the Kingdom. He came alongside me, carried me, comforted me, and protected me until I was able to walk fully into healing. I am so grateful that I did not allow my pain to steal God's Glory. He promises to never leave or forsake us. My prayer is that you apprehend this truth and that it be firmly implanted in your heart.

SCRIPTURE FOR MEDITATION

Isaiah 43:2 (NIV)

When you pass through the waters, I will be with you;
And when you pass through the rivers, they will not sweep you;
When you walk through the fire, you will not be burned; the flames will not set you ablaze.

TEN

FINDING YOUR SELF WORTH

"Your value is far above that of rubies. You are priceless to Him."

One day, I had the pleasure of having breakfast with a young lady who moved into the area as a professor at one of our local colleges. I met her through our church fellowship. She asked me, "Miss Lisa, what do you enjoy doing? What is your passion?" As I was pondering, she continued to speak. "I think it's hard for older women to embrace their passion. They are often burdened with generations of weight that are not their own. It seems too much of a luxury to follow after passion. You have raised your children; you deserve the luxury of passion." She went on to admonish me not to just lean on what I knew how to do, on what was comfortable. She said I deserved to follow my passion. "If you take a chance," she said, "you might stumble upon something fantastic! Remember, Miss Lisa, it's about diligence and worth. Be diligent in your pursuit and know your worth!"

That is my charge to you, dear reader. That you would be diligent in the pursuit of your intended life, in the things that you are passionate about. I hope that you come to know your worth! Just like I looked over my sweater and assessed its worth, the Lord looks over you and me. He runs His eyes over our lives and sees the flaws and the marred places. In the same way that I reflected on the tears, hopes, and dreams that I had knit into the fabric, His son's blood is flowing in us. In the same way that I could not leave that sweater in its unredeemed state, Father God will also not leave us in our unredeemed state. We can submit to His redesign. He can make us over again by making us new in Him.

This is what our God thinks of you according to Psalm 139:13-15 (NIV): "For you created my inmost being; you knit me together in my mother's womb. 14 I praise you because I am fearfully and wonderfully made; your works are wonderful, I know that full well. 15 My frame was not hidden from you when I was made in the secret place when I was woven together in the depths of the earth."

Your value is far above that of rubies. You are priceless to Him. For you, and you alone, the Lord Jesus Christ willfully went to the cross to sacrifice His life for yours. For you, dear reader, and you alone did the sinless one take all of the sins of the world upon Himself. For you, precious one, and for you alone, did He give up His mortal life, taste death, and overcome it. Jesus died for our sake and for the sake of all who will accept Him as Lord and Savior. There is a life that He intended for you; it is confirmed in His Word. I admonish you to press for the intended life that He died for you to have! Long for it and be diligent in your pursuit of it! Don't be derailed by the deceits of the liar. Settle yourself in your identity. Ground yourself into what God has called and prepared you to do.

There is a strategy that I employ that you may find useful. Whenever I see that I am having difficulties in my life, or that my mindset is not lining up with the word, I start to search for the lie in my heart. If I'm off track, there has to be a place where I have inadvertently agreed with a lie, come into partnership with it, and allowed it to dictate my actions. Find the lie! Rebuke it and come out of agreement with it. Replace any lies with the truth of God. Meditate on that truth until your soul believes it, and all residue of the voice of the liar is washed away. Then, repent for believing those lies, and get back on track. That's it! That's the whole formula.

PRAYER

Father, thank You for loving me. Thank You for being mindful of me. Even on my worst days, You love me. There is no place that I can go that You are not there. Your word says if I go up to the heavens, You are there;

if I make my bed in the depths, you are there. Even there your hand will guide me; Your right hand will hold me fast. Your love for me is unfathomable. Thank You for your tender mercies being new every morning.

Father, help me to know Your plan for me. Help me to understand how to put Your plan for me into action. I want to be a doer of your Word, not just one who hears. I choose to be in the center of Your will for my life. I repent for any place that I have agreed with the accuser regarding my life. I know that he comes only to steal, to kill, and to destroy. Thanks be to Jesus, who has come that I would have life and that more abundantly. An abundant life is what I desire. I want abundant life in You. It is in You that I live and breathe and have my being. So, I submit my life to You Father. Use me as your willing vessel. I choose to live a life that glorifies You and advances your kingdom. This is my earnest desire. I bless and exalt Your Name. Be magnified in the heavens! Be magnified on the earth! Be magnified in my life! In Jesus' name, I pray. Amen.

SCRIPTURE FOR MEDITATION

Ephesians 3:20-21 (NIV)

Now to him who is able to do immeasurably more than all we ask or imagine, according to his power that is at work within us, to him be glory in the church and in Christ Jesus throughout all generations, for ever and ever! Amen.

EPILOGUE

The Unraveled Sweater Introduced

"Do not remember the former things,

Nor consider the things of old. Behold, I will do a new thing, Now it shall spring forth;

Shall you not know it? I will even make a road in the wilderness And rivers in the desert.

Isaiah 43:18-19 (NKJV)

I had taken the plunge, untied the final knot, and started to unravel my unflattering sweater. I felt liberated, free, and unencumbered! As each stitch disengaged from the one before it, expectation filled the room. I felt strong and courageous, and oddly mischievous. I felt as if I was doing something unexpected and so unlike the predictable pattern I adopted. I continued to tug on the yarn and unravel the stitches. All was going along pretty well, and then it happened— I ran upon a stitch that was stuck, and it didn't want to come loose. I tugged on the yarn a little harder, and I could see the fibers stretching. Since I didn't want to damage it, I stopped and took a moment to see why I met resistance. Upon inspection, I could see that the stitch had been knit a little awkwardly, and it had created a little knot. I took a moment to pick it apart and free it before I could move on.

Running into that first obstacle caused me to pause for a moment. The yarn that I unraveled was sitting in a pile next to me. As I glanced at it, I became concerned that it might start to get tangled. As much as I was enjoying the unraveling, I realized I needed to plan this out so that my efforts to deconstruct the sweater did not inadvertently destroy the yarn or render it unusable.

I wound up the small section of yarn into a ball and decided I needed to do a bit of research about unraveling a sweater. Was there a process for re-purposing yarn? Were there best practices on how to maintain its integrity so that it could be successfully used for another purpose? Let's grab another cup of tea and a second slice of pound cake, and I'll share what I learned about the deconstruction and reimagining of sweaters and lives.

"The Original Unflattering Sweater"

Made in the USA
Monee, IL
13 November 2021

82001329R00039